Indian Tribes of North America Coloring Book

Peter F. Copeland

DOVER PUBLICATIONS, INC., New York

Introduction

THE ANCESTORS OF the native Americans whom we call Indians arrived in North America from Asia perhaps as early as fifty thousand years ago. At that time a land bridge joined North America with Asia where Siberia met Alaska. On their journeys in the new land these wandering bands of Stone Age hunters, armed with flint-tipped spears, encountered mastodons, giant sloths, woolly mammoths and other forms of prehistoric life now long extinct.

More and more Asians crossed the land bridge to North America and drove the original arrivals farther inland. Gradually, over a period of some twenty thousand years, these people settled North, Central and South America, from Alaska and the Canadian Arctic south through Mexico and the islands of the Caribbean Sea all the way to the Straits of Magellan.

During these millennia they adapted themselves to the vast new world of North America as hunters, farmers, fishermen and warriors. These early Americans evolved in diverse directions. They were not all alike in appearance. Some were tall, others short; some had long heads, others had round heads; some were light-skinned, others dark-skinned. In addition, many different languages developed in different regions of the country. And the societies that developed over so many centuries were as different from one another as the habitats of the forest-dwelling Eastern Woodlands tribes were from those of the hunter-gatherers of the southwestern deserts and plains.

The European exploration and settlement of North America brought about the destruction of the unique American cultures that had developed over many thousands of years. Had it not been for the determination of the European conquerors to destroy them and occupy their lands, the fascinating world of the native North Americans might still exist today in its original colorful cultural diversity.

PETER COPELAND

Copyright © 1990 by Dover Publications, Inc.
All rights reserved under Pan American and International Copyright Conventions.

Published in Canada by General Publishing Company, Ltd., 30 Lesmill Road, Don Mills, Toronto, Ontario.

Indian Tribes of North America Coloring Book is a new work, first published by Dover Publications, Inc., in 1990.

DOVER *Pictorial Archive* SERIES

This book belongs to the Dover Pictorial Archive Series. You may use the designs and illustrations for graphics and crafts applications, free and without special permission, provided that you include no more than four in the same publication or project. (For permission for additional use, please write to Dover Publications, Inc., 31 East 2nd Street, Mineola, N.Y. 11501.) However, republication or reproduction of any illustration by any other graphic service whether it be in a book or in any other design resource is strictly prohibited.

International Standard Book Number: 0-486-26303-7

Manufactured in the United States of America
Dover Publications, Inc., 31 East 2nd Street, Mineola, N.Y. 11501

Algonkian-speaking Indians of North Carolina in 1590. The tribes of the Algonkian-speaking people originally occupied a vast area of North America from the Rocky Mountains to the Atlantic Ocean. Most of the Algonkians lived in bark-covered wigwams like those in the background. This scene, which shows two Indians eating, was copied from a drawing done by John White in the late sixteenth century.

1

Timucua Indians of 1591. Portraits of these Indians of Florida appeared in a book published in Europe in 1591. They were hunters and fishers who lived in towns surrounded by stockades. Their religious ceremonies included human sacrifice. Both men and women were sometimes tattooed on their faces and bodies. The center figure was described as a "Florida Chief." The Timucua became extinct sometime before 1800, following invasions by Creek Indians and English settlers.

New England Indians of 1665. On the left is the great Wampanoag chief King Philip; on the right, Ninigret, chief of the Narraganset Indians of Rhode Island. The two hunting and farming tribes of Algonkian-speaking Indians were largely massacred in the disastrous war launched by King Philip in 1675 in response to ill treatment by the white settlers. This was the sad end of the friendship that began in 1620 between the newly arrived Pilgrims and King Philip's father, Massasoit.

3

Mohawk warriors of 1710. Four Indian "kings" of the Iroquois confederation visited London in 1710: three Mohawks and one Mohican. The city dwellers were fascinated and frightened by their strange appearance and tattoos. The four kings returned to the eastern wood-lands loaded with such gifts as the gold-edged scarlet cloak seen on the Indian on the left. The Mohawks were from New York State, where they raised corn, hunted and fished. The man on the right holds a ball-headed war club.

Iroquois warrior of 1787. The united Iroquois nation—consisting of the Mohawk, Oneida, Onondaga, Cayuga, Seneca, and Tuscarora tribes—extended from New York State through Pennsylvania to northern Ohio and into Canada. Its center was the area of the eastern Great Lakes and the St. Lawrence River.

Though the tribes tended to be warlike, they preserved their confederation for two centuries, up until the American Revolution. This woman's dress shows the great change that occurred in Iroquois costume some years later, after the introduction of woven materials in the early nineteenth century.

Seneca Indians of 1800. The Senecas lived in western New York and eastern Ohio. Their great chief Red Jacket, seen on the right, led some of the Iroquois tribes as allies of the British in the American Revolution, which resulted in the destruction of the Seneca villages. The long, fringed hunting shirts seen here were worn by Indians who had adopted the use of woven cloth in the late eighteenth and early nineteenth centuries.

Seminole Indians of 1825. The Seminoles were Creek Indians who moved into Florida and were joined by runaway slaves. Led by such war chiefs as Billy Bowlegs, they resisted the forces of the Army and Navy in wars that lasted more than ten years and cost the United States more than any other Indian war. Driven into the Everglades, most of the Seminoles finally gave up and allowed themselves to be moved to the West; however, it is the proven claim of part of the tribe that they never surrendered to the United States.

Cherokees at the time of the "Trail of Tears." The home of the Cherokees was the mountainous area of western North Carolina and eastern Tennessee, where they lived in towns of 30–60 log cabins. In 1835 a small minority signed a treaty deeding away their land to the United States. With the winter of 1838 approaching, they were driven from their homeland and forced on a brutal march, the so-called "Trail of Tears," into the Indian territory of Oklahoma. Four thousand of the 18,000 Cherokees died on the march to the West. These Cherokees wear the dress adopted by the tribe at the time of their removal to Oklahoma.

Choctaw women boiling hominy. The Choctaws and the Cherokees were two of the "Five Civilized Tribes" of the southeastern United States. The Choctaws came from Mississippi; like the other four tribes, they were forced to leave their lands and move to Oklahoma in the 1830s. They were skillful farmers. The tribal dress of these modern Choctaw women reflects the influence of white women's dress styles adopted by the tribeswomen of the last century.

A Creek brave of 1834. The Creeks, another of the "Five Civilized Tribes," occupied present-day Georgia and Alabama. The Creeks dominated the Cherokees and Choctaws in the confederation of southeastern tribes. Creek homes were log cabins, in imitation of the white settlers, whom they had first met in 1538. The moccasins and leggings of this brave are of leather, and his fringed shirt is made of striped blanket cloth.

Athabaskan hunters of the far North in 1846. These warriors are of the Kutchin people, members of the widespread Athabaskan group, hunters, warriors and builders of birchbark canoes. The lands of the Athabaskans extended from Lake Athabaska in central Canada to British Columbia and the Yukon River in Alaska; the Kutchins lived in the evergreen forests of the Yukon Territory. The caribou-skin shirts of these hunters are decorated with shells.

Northern Algonkin village scene. This village was in eastern Canada. The wigwams are covered with elm bark. In the background are birchbark canoes. These

Indians are shown dressed in skins, as they were before the arrival of the settlers. The woman in the center is grinding corn in a log mortar. Northern Algonkins wove blankets, made straw baskets and harvested maple sap for syrup in the spring.

13

A Huron encampment in 1845. At this village on the Canadian shores of Lake Huron, we see tepees and canoes covered with birchbark. Birchbark was an essential element in the lives of northern Indians. The heaviest bark, peeled in the spring, was used in the building of canoes; small pieces of bark were used to make torches, buckets, pots and cradles. The Hurons— farmers, fur traders and fishers—were enemies of the Iroquois confederation and were driven from their lands by the Iroquois more than once before the United States forced them to move to Kansas and Oklahoma.

Sauk and Fox warriors of 1834. The Sauk and Fox were a tribe of the Algonkian nation from eastern Wisconsin which moved south to the Mississippi River region before 1800. Originally they were two tribes, which had become one by the close of the Black Hawk War of 1832. The Sauk and Fox were a woodland people who lived in bark-covered lodges, moving to the prairies in warm weather to hunt bison.

Osage Indians of 1804. The Osage were hunter-gatherers whose homeland lay in Missouri and Arkansas. After the adoption of the horse in the early 1700s, the Osage became great buffalo hunters. They were also noted warriors, who often fought with the neighboring Pawnees and Comanches. The warrior's head shown in the inset is shaven and the remaining comb of hair is augmented by a scarlet crest of horsehair.

Ottawa and Chippewa warriors of 1800. These tribes were both members of the Algonkian confederation. The ancient homeland of the Chippewas (also known as Ojibwas) lay along the northern fringes of the Great Lakes, Wisconsin and Minnesota. They were great fur trappers and traders who early adopted the white man's weapons. One of the great Indian leaders of the eighteenth century was Pontiac, a chief of the Ottawa tribe who created a confederacy with the Chippewas and Potawatomis to fight the British in the 1760s. Like other Algonkian peoples, the Chippewa practiced tattooing.

An Iowa chief and woman of 1844. White Cloud was a chief of the Iowa Indians, a small tribe that, by 1836, had been pushed out of its ancient homeland, the territory that would become the state of Iowa. He is shown here wearing a necklace of bear claws and a headdress probably made of porcupine quills. The woman was called Strutting Pigeon.

A *Kansa brave of 1840.* The Kansa people were both buffalo hunters and farmers of the prairies and woodlands. They were a Siouan-speaking tribe, culturally akin to the Osage, the Omaha and the Ponca peoples of the Midwest. The Kansa Indians occupied an area that included parts of present-day Kansas, Oklahoma and western Missouri. The tomahawk seen here is a typical example of those carried by Indians of the midwestern plains. The handle is decorated with a multitude of small brass tacks.

Pawnee tribal leaders of 1865. The Pawnees were farmers of the Great Plains. Their villages were situated along the rivers of Nebraska. They grew crops in the summer and in the fall set out on horseback to hunt buffalo on the plains. In the Indian wars of the 1870s, the Pawnees furnished scouts to the U.S. Army, which was fighting the Sioux.

Indian warfare on the Great Plains. These warriors from rival war parties, as well as their ponies, are embellished with warpaint and armed in the fashion of Plains warriors before the adoption of firearms. A Cree warrior looses an arrow at a Crow warrior who is about to hurl his feathered lance. Both Indians hold shields covered with tough buffalo hide.

22

Hidatsa Dog Soldier and Assiniboin warrior of 1830.
The Hidatsa tribe came originally from the banks of the
Missouri River. This Dog Soldier—a member of a sepa-
rate band of warriors—wears an elaborate feathered
headdress and is armed with a tomahawk of the type
called the "Missouri War hatchet." A scalp hangs from
his belt. The Assiniboin warrior is from a tribe of the
Sioux people of the northern plains. He wears a buffalo
robe and carries a painted shield of buffalo hide.

Cheyenne women at work. The top and left-hand illustrations show steps in the preparation of a buffalo skin for clothing. The woman at the top is giving the skin its first cleaning; at the left another woman is scraping off the hair to produce leather smooth enough for a robe, a shirt, or leggings. The woman at the right is cooking in a "paunch pot," a container made of the stomach of the buffalo. She is boiling water by heating stones in the fire and then dropping them into the water.

A travois of the Northern Plains Indians. The travois was the principal means of transporting household goods, camp equipment, small children and sick or injured people. Before the adoption of the horse, Indians used dogs to haul the travois. By the 1890s the white man's wheeled wagon had largely replaced it.

A Comanche warrior of 1855. The Comanches traveled south from the Rocky Mountains in the early eighteenth century to become famed horsemen on the Texas plains. Comanche war parties in the nineteenth century raided caravans and wagon teams along the Santa Fe Trail, making travel hazardous throughout their territory.

Crow horsemen of 1845. The Crows moved across the Missouri River and into the rolling grassland along the Yellowstone River in the early eighteenth century. After acquiring the horse, they became mounted warriors and drove the Shoshone out of the valley and mountain country south of the Yellowstone. There they became masters of some of the finest game country in the West. The Crows were great hunters, but first and foremost they were warriors. In their religious rituals they achieved supernatural visions through fasting and self-torture.

Apache hunters of 1840. The Apaches of New Mexico and Arizona were a warlike people who lived in scattered camps composed of wickiups, brush-covered huts that resembled overturned baskets. They used powerful bows reinforced with sinew. The Apache women farmed small garden plots and made baskets. Under the chiefs Cochise and Geronimo, they fought the white invaders long and fiercely.

Paiute Indians of Arizona in 1855. The Southern Paiutes lived in hard, desolate desert country. Their way of life was poor and primitive. The women spent their lives gathering seeds and berries and digging for roots with sticks in the parched desert ground. The men hunted antelope, rabbits, lizards, rats, caterpillars and grasshoppers. The Paiutes lived in primitive wickiups and were constantly on the move, in an unending search for food.

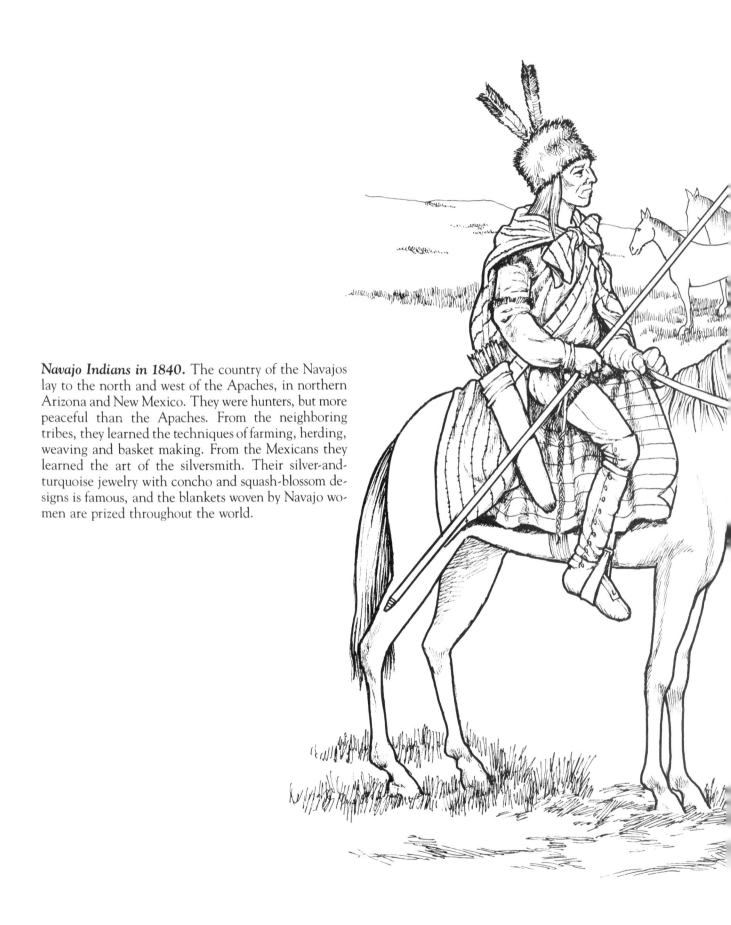

Navajo Indians in 1840. The country of the Navajos lay to the north and west of the Apaches, in northern Arizona and New Mexico. They were hunters, but more peaceful than the Apaches. From the neighboring tribes, they learned the techniques of farming, herding, weaving and basket making. From the Mexicans they learned the art of the silversmith. Their silver-and-turquoise jewelry with concho and squash-blossom designs is famous, and the blankets woven by Navajo women are prized throughout the world.

Mohave Indians of 1860. The lands of the Mohaves lay on the fertile banks of the Colorado River on the Arizona–California border. The Mohaves, unlike most other of the southwestern tribes, were farmers. They frequently engaged in warfare with neighboring tribes. Both men and women were elaborately tattooed.

A Hopi pueblo. The Hopi Indians live in northern Arizona. Since ancient times they have built multistoried pueblo dwellings that are actually fortified towns, some of which have been continuously occupied for many hundreds of years. The Hopis are a peaceful people—farmers, potters, basket makers and weavers.

Hupa Indians of northern California. The Hupa people came from the Trinity River Valley of northern California. They were hunters and fishermen, skilled wood-workers and builders of dugout canoes. The man in this picture holds a powerful, broad, flat hunting bow made of yew wood.

Big Head dancers. The Big Heads were members of a secret society that flourished among Indians of central California. They believed that, if their dance ever were to cease being performed continuously from October to May, the world would disintegrate. The dance was performed in their ceremonial round lodge. The slender rods of the headdress shown here support poppies.

A chief of the southern Utes, 1867. The Utes were originally a food-gathering tribe from the mountains of Colorado. They adopted the horse after 1800 and moved into buffalo country, becoming Plains Indians. This is Ouray, a chief of the southern Utes who sold off portions of the tribal lands to the white settlers of Utah.

Nez Percé Indians, 1885. These Indians were called "Pierced-Nose" by early French explorers, as some of the warriors wore rings in their noses. This custom was long abandoned by 1850. The Nez Percé were salmon fishers before acquiring horses. They became successful horse breeders and traders in their home territory in Idaho, where they developed the famous Appaloosa horse, and they rode them in pursuit of bison. Chief Joseph, seen at the left, led his people in a valiant but disastrous war against invading whites in 1877. At lower right is seen a papoose bound to a cradleboard.

Naskapi hunter of 1805. In the far Canadian north-land between James Bay and the Labrador Sea live the Algonkian-speaking Naskapi people. They are hunters of caribou, moose, beaver and bear. In earlier years their wanderings brought them into contact with the Eskimos (or Inuit), with whom they waged many wars.

Flathead Indians of 1850. The Flatheads were a tribe of the Salish people. Their homeland was in southern Montana, where they hunted bison and often battled with the Plains Indians. The flattened shape of the forehead was an intentional disfiguration done in infancy by tying a board to the infant's padded head as it lay bound to the cradle. The women wove blankets using wool from a species of domestic dog. The man pictured here is Big Knife, a Flathead chief; he carries an eagle-wing fan.

Salish bowmen. The Salish were a large group of north-western tribes which included the Flatheads. They lived in the grasslands and forest of the inland plateau.

The men often went naked in the summer, when the tribes roved in search of fishing and gathering grounds. They were master builders of huge dugout canoes.

Chilkat dancers. These Northwest Coast Indians are performing the "Medicine Mask Dance." Two dancers wear elaborate ceremonial robes made of mountain-goat wool and cedar-bark twine, designed by the men and woven by the women of the tribe. Each one of the cloaks takes a year in the weaving. The Chilkats live on the Alaskan coast.

Index of Tribes and Societies

Algonkian-speaking	1	Iroquois	5
Algonkin	12–13	Kansa	19
Apache	30	Kutchin	11
Assiniboin	24	Mohave	34
Athabaskan	11	Mohawk	4
Big Head society	37	Narraganset	3
Cherokee	8	Naskapi	40–41
Cheyenne	25	Navajo	32–33
Chilkat	44–45	Nez Percé	39
Chippewa	17	Ojibwa	17
Choctaw	9	Osage	16
Comanche	28	Ottawa	17
Cree	22–23	Paiute	31
Creek	10	Pawnee	20–21
Crow	22–23, 29	Salish	43
Dog Soldier	24	Sauk and Fox	15
Flathead	42	Seminole	7
Hidatsa	24	Seneca	6
Hopi	35	Timucua	2
Hupa	36	Ute	38
Huron	14	Wampanoag	3
Iowa	18		